better together*

* This book is best read together, grownup and kid.

a
kids
book
about

a kids book about

by Jessica Jackley

A Kids Book About
Editor Emma Wolf
Head of Design Rick DeLucco
Publisher Jelani Memory

DK
Senior Production Editor Jennifer Murray
Senior Production Controller Louise Minihane
Managing Editor Hazel Eriksson
Publishing Director Mark Searle

This American Edition, 2025
Published in the United States by DK Publishing,
a Division of Penguin Random House LLC
1745 Broadway, 20th Floor, New York, NY 10019

25 26 27 28 29 10 9 8 7 6 5 4 3 2 1
001—351834—Nov/2025

Published in Great Britain by Dorling Kindersley Limited.

ISBN 979-8-2171-2894-5

Printed and bound in China

www.dk.com

akidsco.com

To Cyrus, Jaspar, Asa, and Soraya—
the greatest gifts of my life.

Intro
for grownups

We often tell kids that sharing is caring. But have you ever stopped to think about what giving really means? It's more than just handing over toys or splitting a snack. Giving can change how we feel, how others feel, and even how our whole world works.

As grownups, we sometimes focus on teaching kids the basics—be polite, work hard, play fair. But giving deserves special attention because it connects to something deeper: how we treat each other and how we build communities where everyone has what they need.

This book isn't just about giving stuff away. It's about opening our hearts, using our talents, and offering our time in ways that make life better for everyone.

My hope is to spark conversations between kids and grownups about generosity, empathy, and how even the smallest acts of giving can create the biggest ripples of change. Let's explore the magic of giving together!

HAVE YOU EVER RECEIVED A GIFT?

Maybe it was for your **birthday**,

a **holiday**,

or some other **special occasion**.

WHAT
DID
YOU
GET?

Something you really wanted,
or needed, or both?

**(Or neither?!
Ugh, not more boring socks!)**

HOW
DID
YOU
FEEL?

Receiving a gift
can make us feel...

happy

thankful

seen

known

cared for

loved

And guess what:

can feel even better.

My name is **Jessica**.

Ever since I was a kid,
I've wanted to help people.

Whether it was my **family, friends, neighbors, or even people I didn't know,** I loved doing things for others that made their day a little better.

Sometimes, I'd find all the spare change I could and give it to a charity or put it in the basket that got passed around at church.

Other times, I'd gather donations of clothing or shoes so I could give them to people in need.

I also gave a lot of my time.

THIS LOOKED LIKE...

helping younger kids
with their schoolwork,

raking leaves
in neighbors' yards,

teaching grownups
how to swim,

bringing food
to people in hospitals,

picking up garbage
at my local park,

and other things like that!

I learned that when I gave,

I FELT
REALLY
GOOD.

When I grew up, I started an organization to help other people give, too, so that everyone could feel as good as I did!

I thought it would be awesome
if someone could lend a little bit of
money to another person anywhere
in the world who needed it—
and then get paid back.

WHAT I BUILT INSPIRED

OF PEOPLE TO SHARE

OF DOLLARS WITH OTHERS!

IONS

IONS

You might have heard about this kind of giving before—**giving money**.

Money is pretty useful
when it comes to helping people
get what they need, like:

enough food,

or **warm clothes**,

or **a good education**,

or **a safe place to call home**.

Did you know that not
everyone has those things...

even though some of us have
so much more than we need?

IT'S
NOT
FAIR.

I believe everyone can and should have what they need.

**When we give,
we can help make that happen.**

You might be thinking to yourself,

"HEY, I'M JUST A KID! I DON'T HAVE A BUNCH OF MONEY TO GIVE!"

THAT'S OK!

Money can be helpful, but it's not the most important thing.

THE MOST IMPORTANT THING YOU CAN GIVE IS...

...YOU.

What does this look like?

WELL, HAVE YOU GIVEN ANY OF THESE TODAY?

A SMILE. A HUG.
YOUR ATTENTION.
YOUR TIME.
YOUR TALENTS.
AN ENCOURAGING WORD.
A TOY OR A BOOK.
A GREAT IDEA.
A SILLY JOKE THAT MADE SOMEONE LAUGH.

Giving is a way
of saying to someone else:

I SEE YOU. YOU ARE IMPORTANT.

When you share a smile,
you are sharing a little bit of joy.

When you give a hug,
you make someone feel loved.

When you pay attention to someone,
you're showing them they matter.

And when you share your great ideas,
you're giving inspiration and hope.

You might even inspire someone else to give too!

Because, believe it or not,

GIOUS!

(Yes, just like yawns or giggles!)

So, why doesn't *everyone* give,
all the time?

Sometimes, people think giving means giving something **up**, or giving something **away**, and ending up with **less**.

But that's not exactly how giving works.

A lot of the time, when you give,

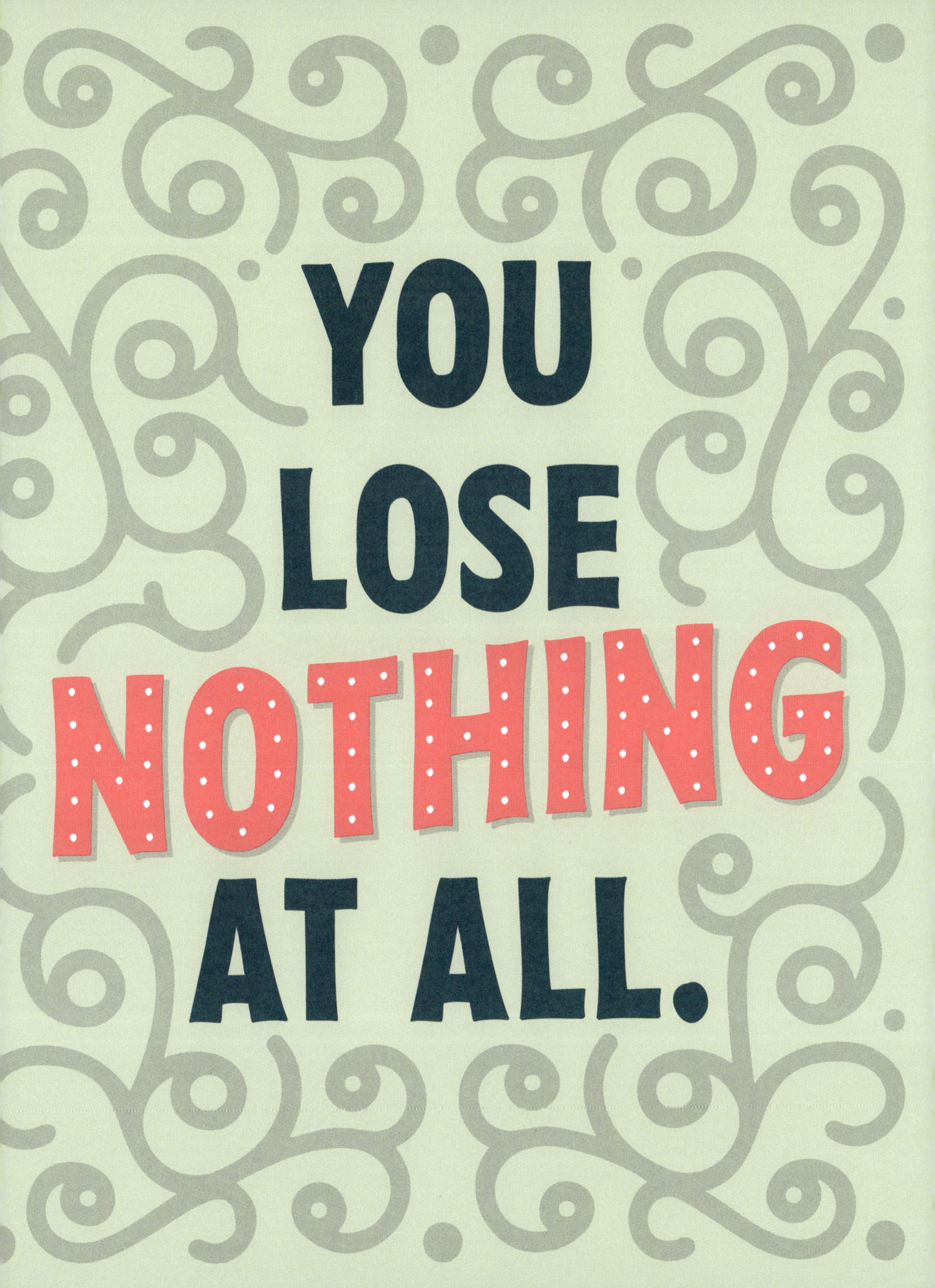
YOU
LOSE
NOTHING
AT ALL.

In fact, you almost always...

GET A LOT BACK.

You might get
a "thank you," a high five,
or that awesome feeling when
you know you've helped someone.

Sometimes, you even end up with...

MORE
THAN
YOU HAD
AT THE
START!

How does that work?!

Maybe you **gain** a new friend,

a stronger community,

or even a changed world.

Giving is absolutely

MAG

CAL!

So, get out there and make
some magic happen.
(FOR REAL!)

WHERE WILL

Do you see a friend
or sibling who looks lonely?

A plant that needs water?

A pet that needs food?

How could you make your
school or neighborhood better?

What could you fix if you tried?

YOU START?

Do you want to help make sure all people have enough food to eat, clean water to drink, and a safe place to live?

Do you care a lot about protecting the earth? How could you learn more about how to help? (Hint: Check out the ideas in the back of this book!)

Maybe just start with the grownup reading this book with you.

I bet they could use a "thank you" or a hug. 🙂

THE WORLD NEEDS

THE WORLD NEEDS

THE WORLD NEEDS

HELPERS.
GIVERS.
YOU.

RESOURCES FOR GIVING

DAY-TO-DAY ACTS OF KINDNESS

Kindness calendar: Create a monthly calendar with simple acts of kindness for each day, like leaving a nice note for someone, helping with chores without being asked, or sharing a toy.

Gratitude jar: Keep a jar where you and your family members can write down things you're grateful for or kind acts you've witnessed. Read them together at the end of each month.

Neighborhood helper: Look for ways to help neighbors—offer to walk a dog, bring in mail, or water plants.

Compliment challenge: Challenge everyone in your family to give at least 3 sincere compliments to different people each day.

Green good deeds: Pick up litter, start a small garden, or set up a bird feeder to practice giving to our environment.

COMMUNITY AND CITYWIDE RESOURCES

Local food banks: Many food banks welcome families for sorting and packing activities. Find your local food bank through Feeding America's website, feedingamerica.org.

Library programs: Check your local library for books about giving and community service, plus volunteer opportunities like reading to younger children.

Animal shelters: Many shelters have programs where kids can help socialize animals or create toys for them.

Family Volunteer Day: Participate in this national day of service (held the Saturday before Thanksgiving) with projects designed for all ages.

Points of Light: Visit pointsoflight.org to find family-friendly volunteer opportunities in your community and access resources designed specifically for young volunteers.

ADDITIONAL RESOURCES

Books about giving: Look for age-appropriate books at your library like *Last Stop on Market Street* or *Those Shoes*.

Family giving traditions: Start traditions like donating a toy for each new toy received, or having a birthday party where guests bring donations instead of gifts.

School service clubs: Participate in school clubs focused on service—or start one if it doesn't exist yet!

Outro
for grownups

Now that we've reached the end of our journey, you might be wondering: What's next? If you're a grownup reading this with a kid, I hope they're bubbling with questions and ideas! They might ask, "How can I start giving right now?"

Embrace these questions. Kids naturally understand fairness and sharing in ways that sometimes surprise us grownups. They see possibilities where we often see complications.

I invite you to look for opportunities to give together. Notice who might need help in your neighborhood. Talk about organizations that support causes you care about. Discuss how giving your time can sometimes matter more than giving things.

Remember that giving isn't just something we do occasionally—it's a way of moving through the world with open hands and hearts. By nurturing this spirit in kids, we help create a generation of people who instinctively ask, "How can I help?" and show up for each other, their communities, and the planet.

The smallest act of kindness today could grow into a lifetime of generosity tomorrow.

About The Author

Jessica Jackley (she/her) builds organizations that solve important problems. She started Kiva, a website where people can lend small amounts of money to help others around the world start businesses. These tiny loans have added up to almost $3 billion since 2005!

Jessica teaches entrepreneurship at the University of Southern California and has created other social businesses too, like Alltruists, which gives families fun ways to volunteer and help others from home. She once worked with Walt Disney Imagineering (the people who design Disney parks!) and has written another book called *Clay Water Brick* about entrepreneurs who started with very little.

Jessica believes everyone deserves a chance to make their dreams come true, even if they don't have much money to start with. She lives in Los Angeles with her husband, Reza, and their 4 kids, who are learning that giving to others is one of life's greatest joys.

www.jessicajackley.com